MAD FOR GEOGRAPHY
CITIES

Edited by
Paola Misesti

Illustrations by
Agnese Baruzzi

CITIES
A WORLD WAITING TO BE DISCOVERED

Geography is a fascinating subject because it allows us to learn about the world around us, from many different points of view.

This book teaches kids about cities and urban planning—that is, the discipline that studies different settlements and areas that have been modified by humans.

Secrets and curiosities about cities are recounted in a story about two young apprentice geographers, Gea and Tom, and an apprentice urban planner, Corby. Through games and activities kids will discover how many types of cities there are, how they've changed over time, their functions, how they're structured, and how they can be made more sustainable.

They'll also learn about a few famous monuments and some very special homes that can be found around the world.

Finally, they'll be able to create their very own future city!

At the end of the book, each reader will be awarded an apprentice urban planner's ribbon.

A Few Notes About the Activities

While all of the activities are presented in the form of fun and practical games, they also provide loads of information and fun facts about the world of cities. The order of the activities is designed to allow children to acquire knowledge gradually and easily, and we therefore recommend that they follow the story page by page.

There's a mixture of simple and more complex activities, making the book engaging and stimulating for children of different ages, without them becoming frustrated or bored.

There will also be materials to cut out and others needed for making things, each accompanied by detailed and illustrated explanations. All of the activities are designed for children to do on their own, but the presence of an adult can be stimulating and supportive, especially for younger children.

Along with the activities, there are eight pages of stickers to use in the book, and all of the solutions can be found in the last few pages.

THIS BOOK IS FOR CHILDREN AGES 7 AND OLDER.

The Future Geographers Club

Hi!
We're Gea and Tom, two aspiring geographers. We love geography and anything to do with studying the earth. Tom loves maps and wants to become a cartographer. We've also brought along our friend Corby. He knows everything about cities and loves urban planning. We all belong to the **Future Geographers Club**.
If you'd like to know more about us, take a look at our membership cards.

Future Geographers Club

NAME:	GEA
LAST NAME:	WELT
AGE:	10
HOBBIES:	GEOGRAPHY, READING, PHOTOGRAPHY, MINERALS
FAVORITE ANIMAL:	PANDA
FAVORITE COLOR:	PURPLE

Future Geographers Club

NAME:	TOM
LAST NAME:	COMPASS
AGE:	11
HOBBIES:	CARTOGRAPHY, VIDEO GAMES
FAVORITE ANIMAL:	CHAMELEON
FAVORITE COLOR:	GREEN

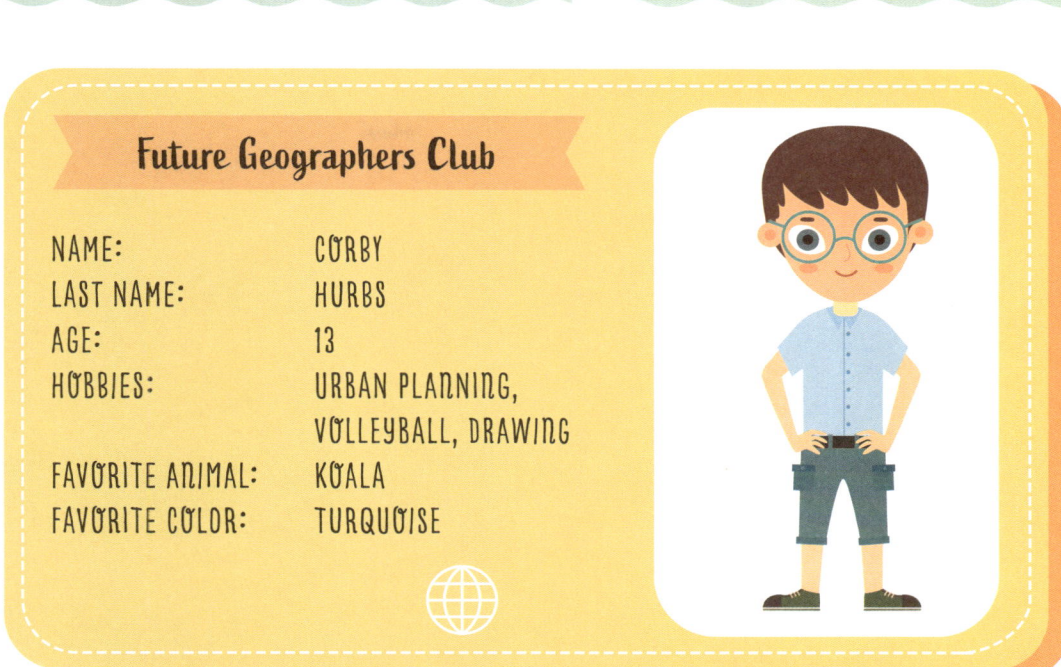

Future Geographers Club

NAME: CORBY
LAST NAME: HURBS
AGE: 13
HOBBIES: URBAN PLANNING, VOLLEYBALL, DRAWING
FAVORITE ANIMAL: KOALA
FAVORITE COLOR: TURQUOISE

WELCOME TO THE CLUB!
YOU CAN JOIN THE FUTURE GEOGRAPHERS CLUB, TOO!
FILL OUT THE MEMBERSHIP CARD BELOW, THEN ATTACH A PHOTO OR DRAWING OF YOURSELF!

Future Geographers Club

NAME: ....
LAST NAME: ....
AGE: ....
HOBBIES: ....
....
FAVORITE ANIMAL: ....
FAVORITE COLOR: ....

Urban Planning

URBAN PLANNING IS THE DISCIPLINE THAT STUDIES CITIES AND DIFFERENT SETTLEMENTS AND AREAS THAT HAVE BEEN MODIFIED BY HUMANS.
A PERSON WHO DOES URBAN PLANNING IS CALLED AN **URBAN PLANNER**.

Spot the Differences

IF YOU LOOK AROUND YOU, YOU'LL SEE THAT THERE ARE VARIOUS TYPES OF LANDSCAPES.

Some are **natural**, composed only of elements found in nature, such as forests, rivers, lakes, mountains, and cliffs.
Others are **anthropic**, which means they've been **modified by humans** according to their needs. You'll see things like dams, cultivated fields, houses, roads, ports, and railways. Look at these two landscapes and spot the differences that make **the natural landscape an anthropic landscape**. How many differences are there?

NATURAL LANDSCAPE

ANTHROPIC LANDSCAPE

WHAT OTHER THINGS CAN HUMANS BUILD THAT CHANGE THE LANDSCAPE? DRAW THEM BELOW.

Rural or Urban?

ANTHROPIC LANDSCAPES CAN BE RURAL OR URBAN.

In an anthropic **rural** landscape, you'll find things like cultivated fields, farms, and irrigation systems.
In an anthropic **urban** landscape, on the other hand, you'll find cities, shopping malls, airports, hospitals, factories, and so on.
Using the stickers in the book, put all the elements shown at the bottom of the page in the correct place in the urban area or the rural area.

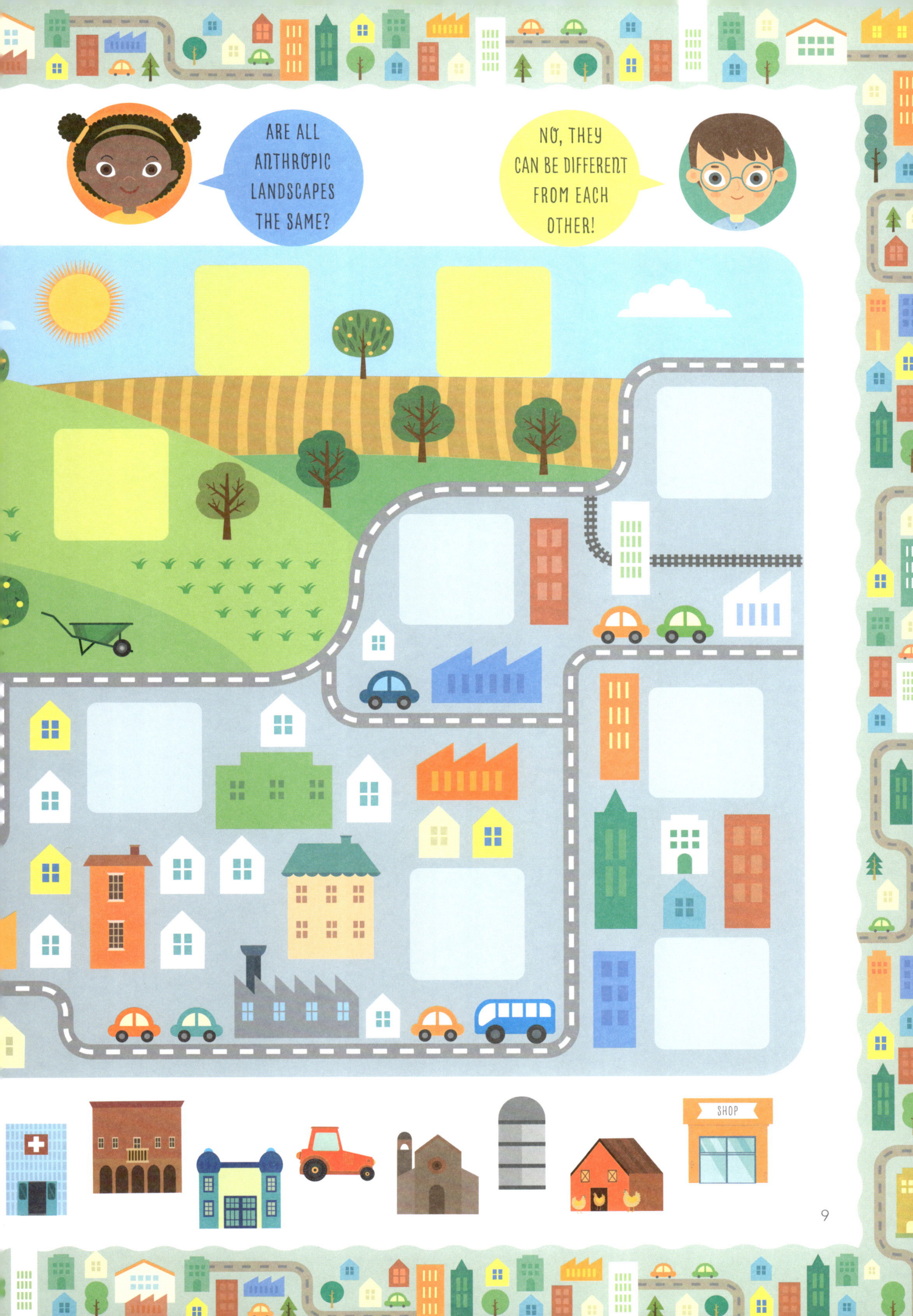

Let's Put Everything in Order

ABOUT 3.5 BILLION PEOPLE, OR HALF OF HUMANITY, LIVE IN CITIES.

SETTLEMENTS ARE BUILT-UP AREAS.

This is where humans live and work. They can be individual houses, like in rural areas, or groups of houses, like in towns and cities. Settlements have different names, depending on their size and how many people live there. Can you help me put the stickers in the correct boxes?

VILLAGE
very few inhabitants

TOWN
more inhabitants

CITY
lots of inhabitants

METROPOLIS
more than 1,000,000 inhabitants

Find the Name!

DID YOU KNOW THERE ARE SOME REALLY HUGE CITIES IN THE WORLD?

They are home to over 10,000,000 inhabitants!
If you want to find out what they're called, find all the listed words hidden in the grid.
Put the remaining letters in the right order to find the name you're looking for!

U	R	B	A	N	P	L	A	N	N	E	R
M	E	T	R	O	P	O	L	I	S	●	●
V	I	L	L	A	G	E	●	●	●	●	M
E	I	N	H	A	B	I	T	E	D	●	●
G	A	R	U	R	A	L	●	●	L	O	P
●	C	O	U	N	T	R	Y	S	I	D	E
B	U	I	L	D	I	N	G	S	●	●	●
G	E	O	G	R	A	P	H	Y	●	●	O
L	I	S	P	L	A	I	N	●	●	●	●

GEOGRAPHY   INHABITED   URBAN PLANNER   VILLAGE   PLAIN   BUILDINGS
RURAL   COUNTRYSIDE   METROPOLIS

_ _ _ _ _ _ _ _ _ _

Here are some huge cities.
Maybe you already know some of them:
SHANGHAI, DELHI, LAGOS, MEXICO CITY...

Conurbation

THIS IS A LATIN TERM COMPOSED OF "CON," MEANING "TOGETHER," AND "URBIS," MEANING "CITY"—THEREFORE IT MEANS A "CLUSTER OF CITIES."

Sometimes a city expands so much that it joins with neighboring towns, a bit like a spreading stain! These towns don't merge with the city, but remain autonomous.
Look at this map and create your own conurbation by joining the various towns with the largest city. Choose which ones you want to be part of your conurbation and leave the others out.

Metropolitan Area

WHEN A METROPOLIS—THAT IS, A VERY LARGE CITY—EXPANDS SO MUCH THAT IT JOINS SMALLER CITIES, WHICH THEN BECOME DEPENDENT ON IT FOR SERVICES, TRANSPORTATION, ECONOMIC ACTIVITIES, AND MUCH MORE, IT IS CALLED A **METROPOLITAN AREA**.

On the map, there is a metropolitan area in which a city depends on the metropolis for 4 services. Find the 4 services that the small city doesn't have and for which the inhabitants must go to the largest city. Finally, put the corresponding stickers in the boxes.

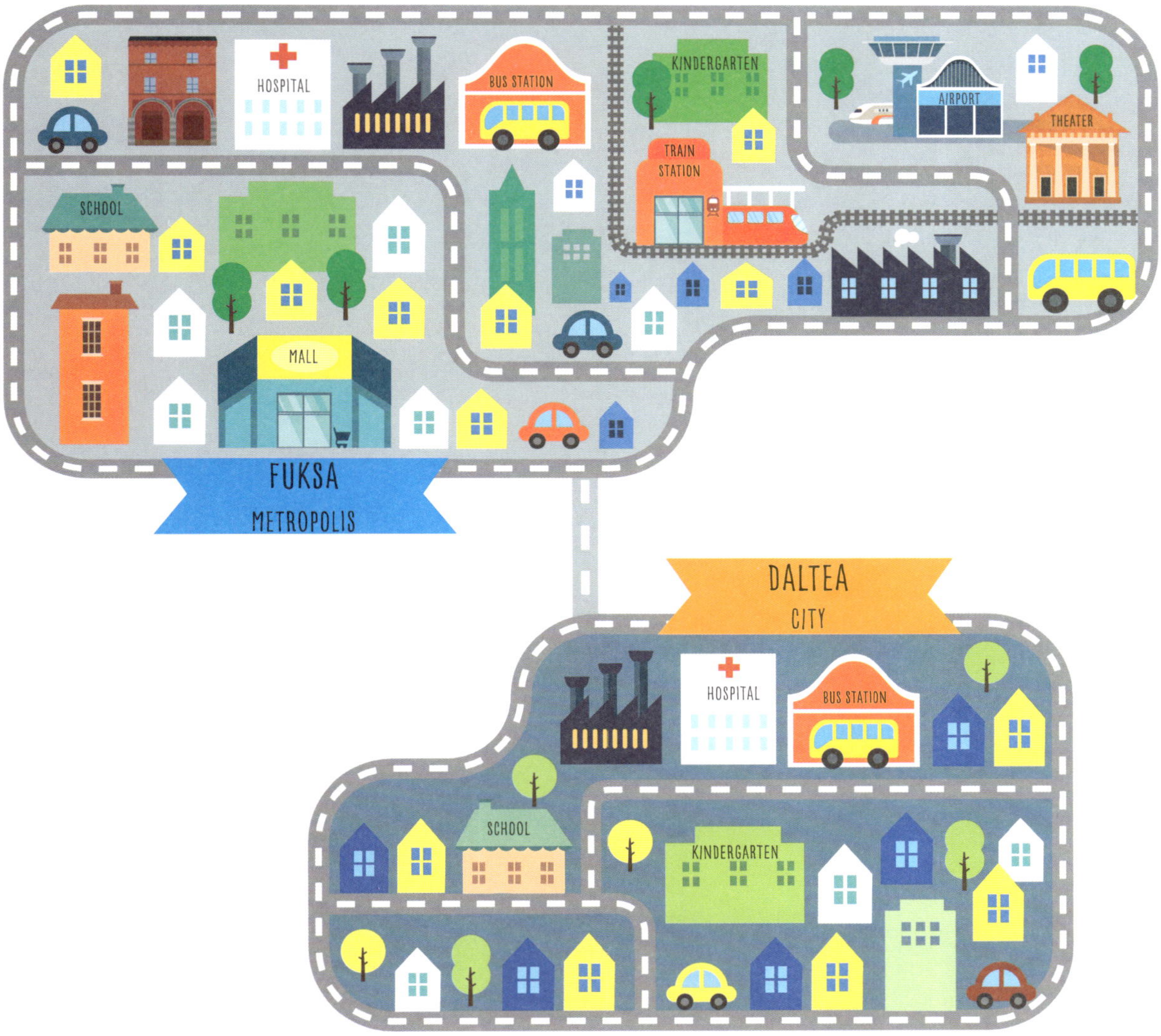

WHICH SERVICES ARE FOUND ONLY IN THE METROPOLIS?

How Many of Us Are There?

DEMOGRAPHY IS THE SCIENCE THAT STUDIES POPULATIONS AND HOW THEY CHANGE OVER TIME. THIS IS DONE THROUGH INDICATORS.

An example would be the number of people who are born in or who have changed cities, or the number of inhabitants in the same area during different time periods. This indicator is called **population density.** Look at these two maps! They show the population density of the same city in different years. The colors indicate the areas where there's low, medium, or high density, depending on whether more or less people live there.

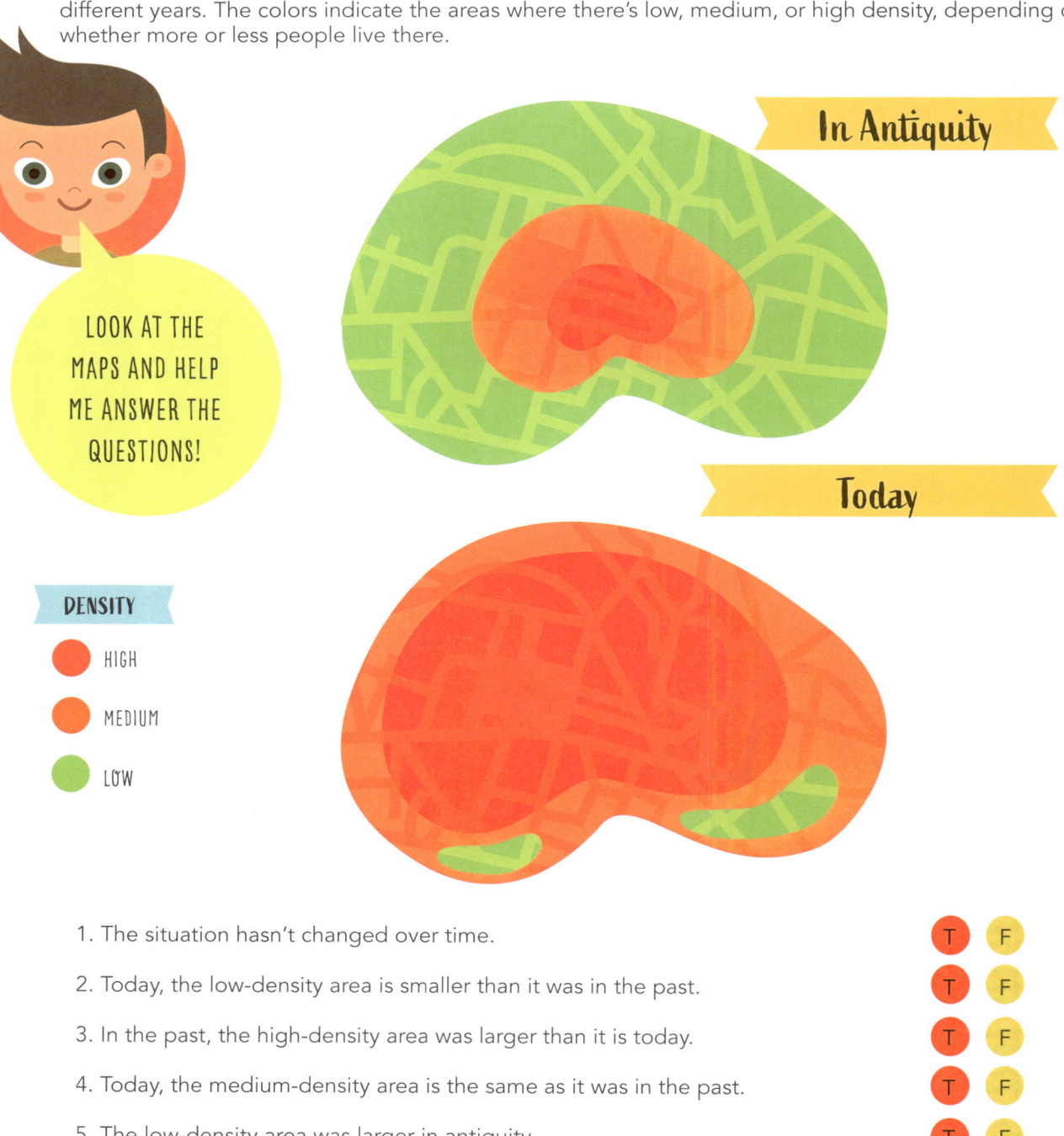

LOOK AT THE MAPS AND HELP ME ANSWER THE QUESTIONS!

DENSITY
- 🟠 HIGH
- 🟧 MEDIUM
- 🟢 LOW

1. The situation hasn't changed over time. T F
2. Today, the low-density area is smaller than it was in the past. T F
3. In the past, the high-density area was larger than it is today. T F
4. Today, the medium-density area is the same as it was in the past. T F
5. The low-density area was larger in antiquity. T F

A Matter of Lines

DEMOGRAPHY ALSO USES **HISTOGRAMS** TO UNDERSTAND HOW A POPULATION IS FORMED OR HOW IT CHANGES OVER TIME.

A **histogram** is a chart of vertical or horizontal bars that visually represents a set of data. The one below represents the population of my city, at the time when my grandparents were children.

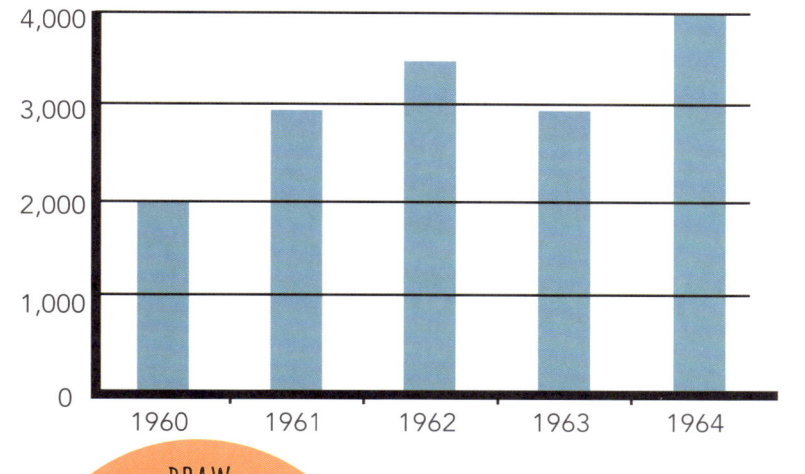

Inhabitants by year

1960 = 2,000
1961 = 3,000
1962 = 3,500
1963 = 3,000
1964 = 4,000

DRAW THE HISTOGRAM FOR THE TIME OF MY GREAT-GRANDPARENTS, 1930-1933, BASED ON THE DATA IN THE KEY.

Inhabitants by year

1930 = 500
1931 = 450
1932 = 450
1933 = 500

A Matter of Numbers

CITIES ARE ALSO CLASSIFIED ACCORDING TO THEIR POPULATION, MEANING THE NUMBER OF INHABITANTS.

Complete the table with the names of the cities, based on the population. Look carefully at the map and the key!

KEY

- ● 3,000,000 INHABITANTS
- ○ 145,000 INHABITANTS
- • 6,500 INHABITANTS
- · 400 INHABITANTS

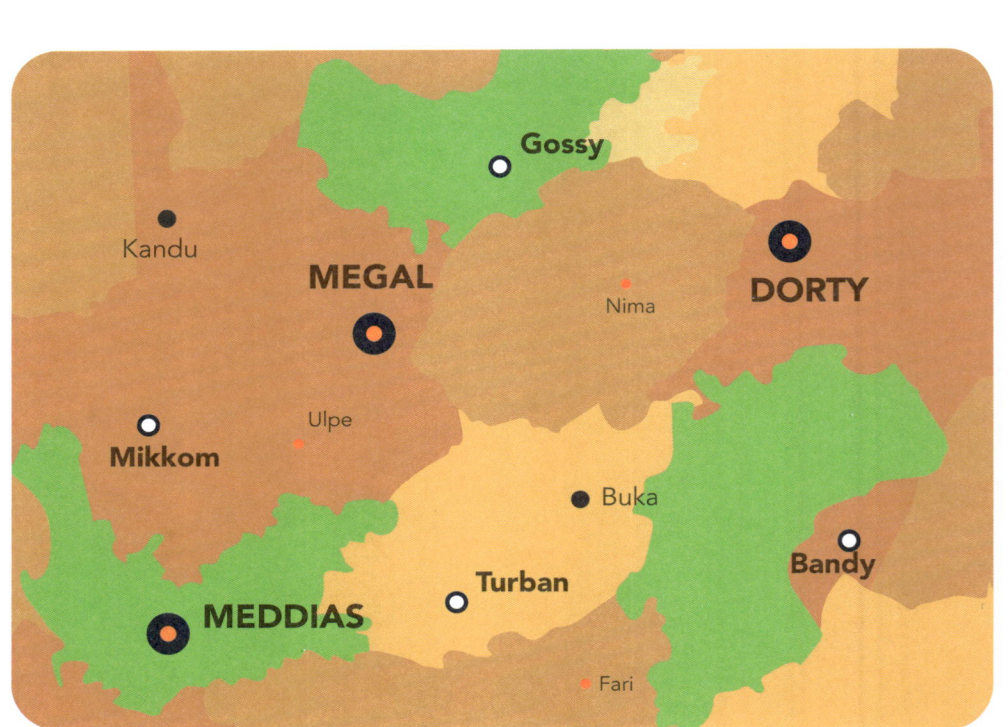

400 INHABITANTS	6,500 INHABITANTS	145,000 INHABITANTS	3,000,000 INHABITANTS
Fari	Buka	....	....
....	....	....	....
....	....	....	....

It's Not All About Numbers!

THERE ARE SOME CITIES IN THE WORLD THAT ARE VERY IMPORTANT NOT BECAUSE OF THEIR SIZE OR THE NUMBER OF INHABITANTS, BUT BECAUSE THEY PERFORM FUNCTIONS THAT ARE KEY TO THE WORLD ECONOMY.

Do you know what they're called? Decrypt the code to find out!

A	B	C	D	E	F	G	H	I	J	K	L	M
13	5	14	20	1	15	4	16	19	22	25	7	6

N	O	P	Q	R	S	T	U	V	W	X	Y	Z
21	18	8	9	3	17	10	2	11	24	23	26	12

___ ___ ___ ___ ___ ___   ___ ___ ___ ___ ___ ___
 4   7   18   5   13   7   14   19   10   19   1   17

PARIS, TOKYO, LONDON, AND NEW YORK are a few examples of these types of cities!

Cities Over Time

CITIES HAVEN'T ALWAYS LOOKED LIKE THEY DO TODAY.

Use the **stickers** to complete the diagram showing how cities have changed over time.

PREHISTORY

PREHISTORY

THE FIRST HUMAN SETTLEMENTS APPEARED IN PREHISTORIC TIMES.

MIDDLE AGES

MODERN ERA

ANTIQUITY

ANTIQUITY

AS THE POPULATION INCREASED AND HUMANS MADE NEW DISCOVERIES, CITIES BECAME LARGER AND CHANGED IN APPEARANCE.

INDUSTRIAL AGE

TODAY

The Functions of a City

ALL THE SPACES IN A CITY HAVE A SPECIFIC PURPOSE TO MEET THE NEEDS OF CITIZENS.

Here are some of a city's key functions:

- **Housing**: places to live, such as houses, apartments, and high-rises.
- **Economic/productive**: spaces in which to produce or sell goods or services, such as industries, shopping malls, stores, offices, and markets.
- **Financial/commercial**: places where economic activities are carried out, such as ports, airports, and banks.
- **Political/administrative**: the seats of political and administrative bodies, such as government buildings, and the police.
- **Services**: places with cultural, recreational, and religious functions, such as schools, movie theaters, libraries, parks, swimming pools, and places of worship.

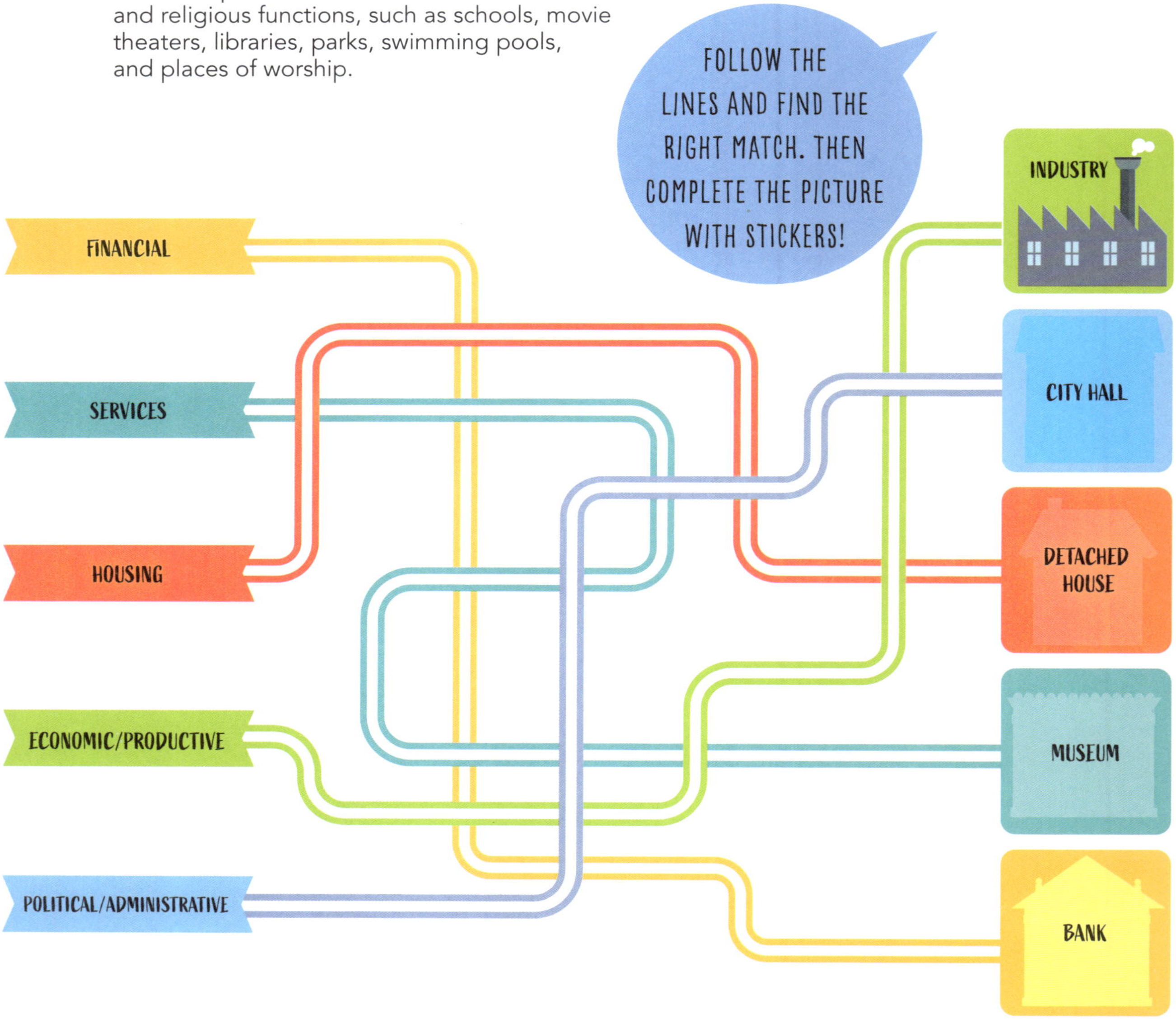

FOLLOW THE LINES AND FIND THE RIGHT MATCH. THEN COMPLETE THE PICTURE WITH STICKERS!

Public or Private?

THERE ARE 2 TYPES OF SPACES IN CITIES: **PUBLIC** AND **PRIVATE**.

Public spaces are places used by the community, such as parks, libraries, museums, and shopping malls.
Private spaces are places intended for family and personal life, such as houses and apartments.

Help me put the corresponding stickers in the correct column, depending on whether they are public or private spaces.

PUBLIC

PRIVATE

21

Where Am I Going?

PUBLIC SPACES PERFORM VARIOUS FUNCTIONS.

Help Gea, Tom, and Corby get to the correct buildings.

The City Tetris

HELP US PUT THESE BUILDINGS ONTO THE MAP ON THE OPPOSITE PAGE.

Compose the buildings with the stickers and find their correct location. Pay attention to their shapes; you can't change them!

THERE MUST NOT BE ANY WHITE SQUARES LEFT ON THE MAP!

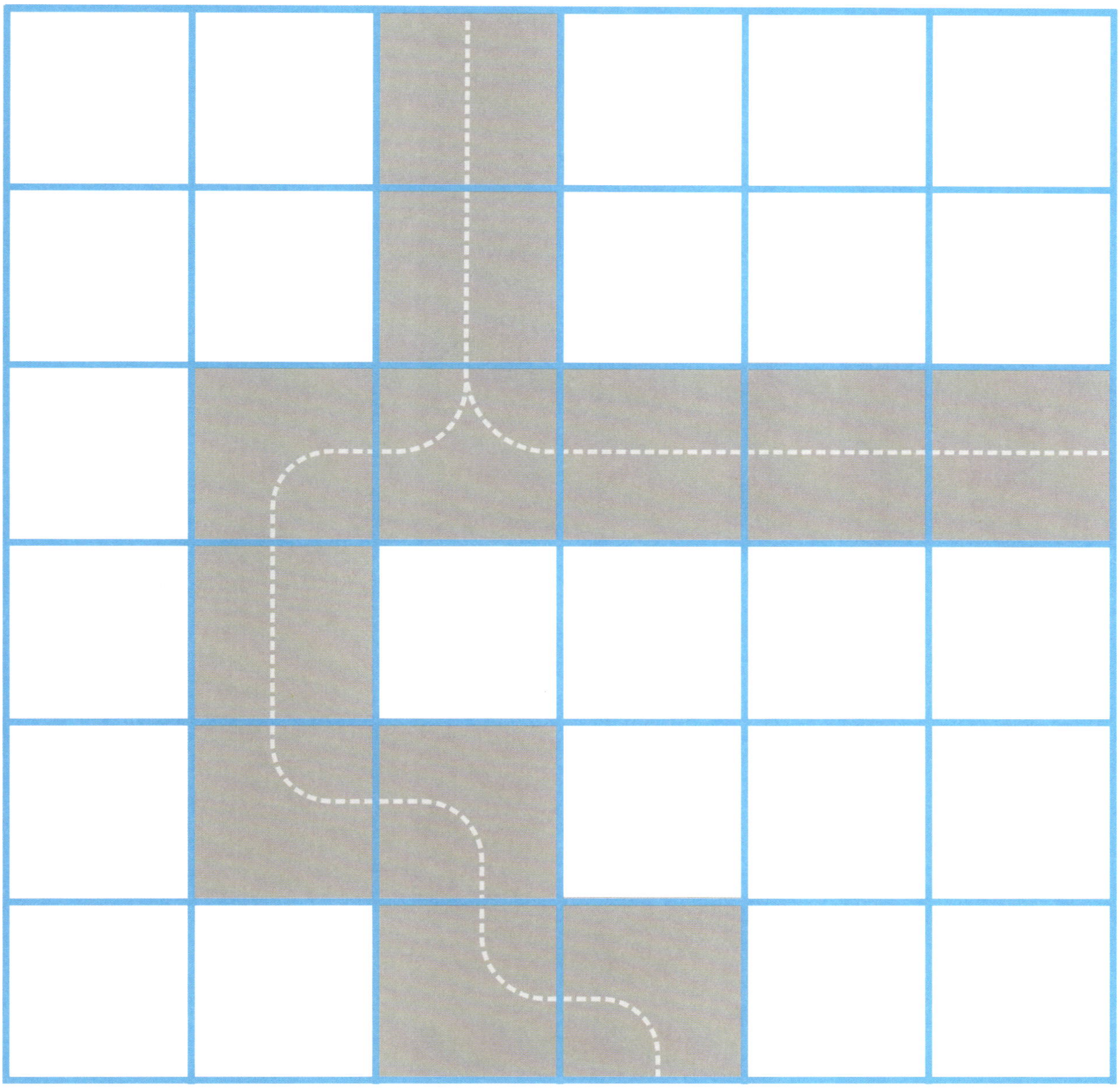

Different Patterns

CITIES ARE MADE UP OF HOUSES, PARKS, STORES, INDUSTRIES, AND BUILDINGS.

They have various patterns when viewed from above; there are 4 that are most common.
Complete the maps with the stickers, then read the descriptions carefully.
Next connect each description to the correct map by drawing a line.

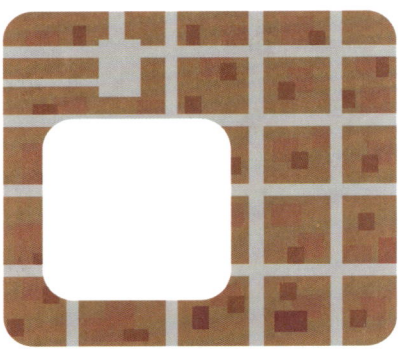

RADIAL CITY
THE MAIN ROADS EXTEND OUTWARD IN VARIOUS DIRECTIONS FROM A CENTER, WHICH EXPANDS TO FORM INCREASINGLY LARGER CIRCLES.

GRID CITY
THE VARIOUS ROADS INTERSECT AT RIGHT ANGLES, FORMING BLOCKS IN THE FORM OF SQUARES OR RECTANGLES.

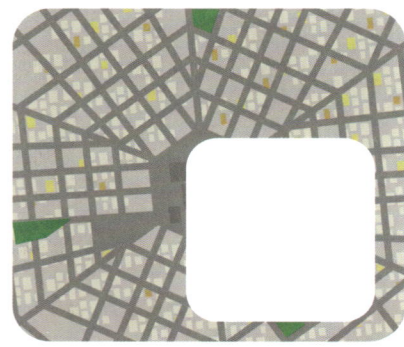

MIXED PLAN CITY
THIS IS A CITY IN WHICH DIFFERENT TYPES OF PLANS HAVE OVERLAPPED.

LINEAR CITY
THIS IS A CITY THAT DEVELOPS ALONG A MAIN ROAD OR COMMUNICATION ROUTE, SUCH AS A RAILWAY OR A WATERWAY.

The City Center

IF WE LOOK AT CITY PLANS IN MORE DETAIL, WE CAN SEE THAT THE TYPE OF BUILDINGS IN AN AREA ARE OFTEN SIMILAR. LOOK AT THESE MAPS!

The city **center** is typically the **oldest** part of a city. Here you will find the oldest buildings, museums, and city hall. Help me find the city center in these plans, and then circle it!

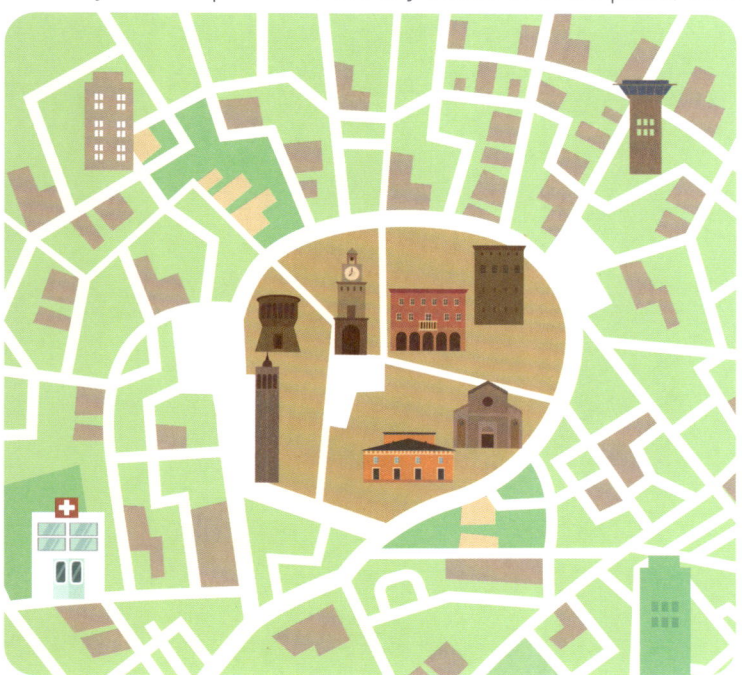

Here's an example

A PLAN is the design of an area viewed from above and reduced in size, maintaining the correct proportions. A city is divided into areas called NEIGHBORHOODS.

Famous Monuments

MANY IMPORTANT MONUMENTS ARE LOCATED IN CITIES. COMPLETE THEM WITH STICKERS!

Some of them are so famous that they identify the city itself.

RIO DE JANEIRO   PARIS   ROME   NEW YORK   AGRA   BEIJING   SYDNEY   ATHENS

OPERA HOUSE ....

FORBIDDEN CITY ....

CHRIST THE REDEEMER ....

ACROPOLIS ....

Residential Districts

IF WE LEAVE THE CITY CENTER, WE'LL FIND A MORE MODERN AREA CALLED THE **RESIDENTIAL** DISTRICT.

Here there are newer homes, as well as offices, stores, schools, and parks.

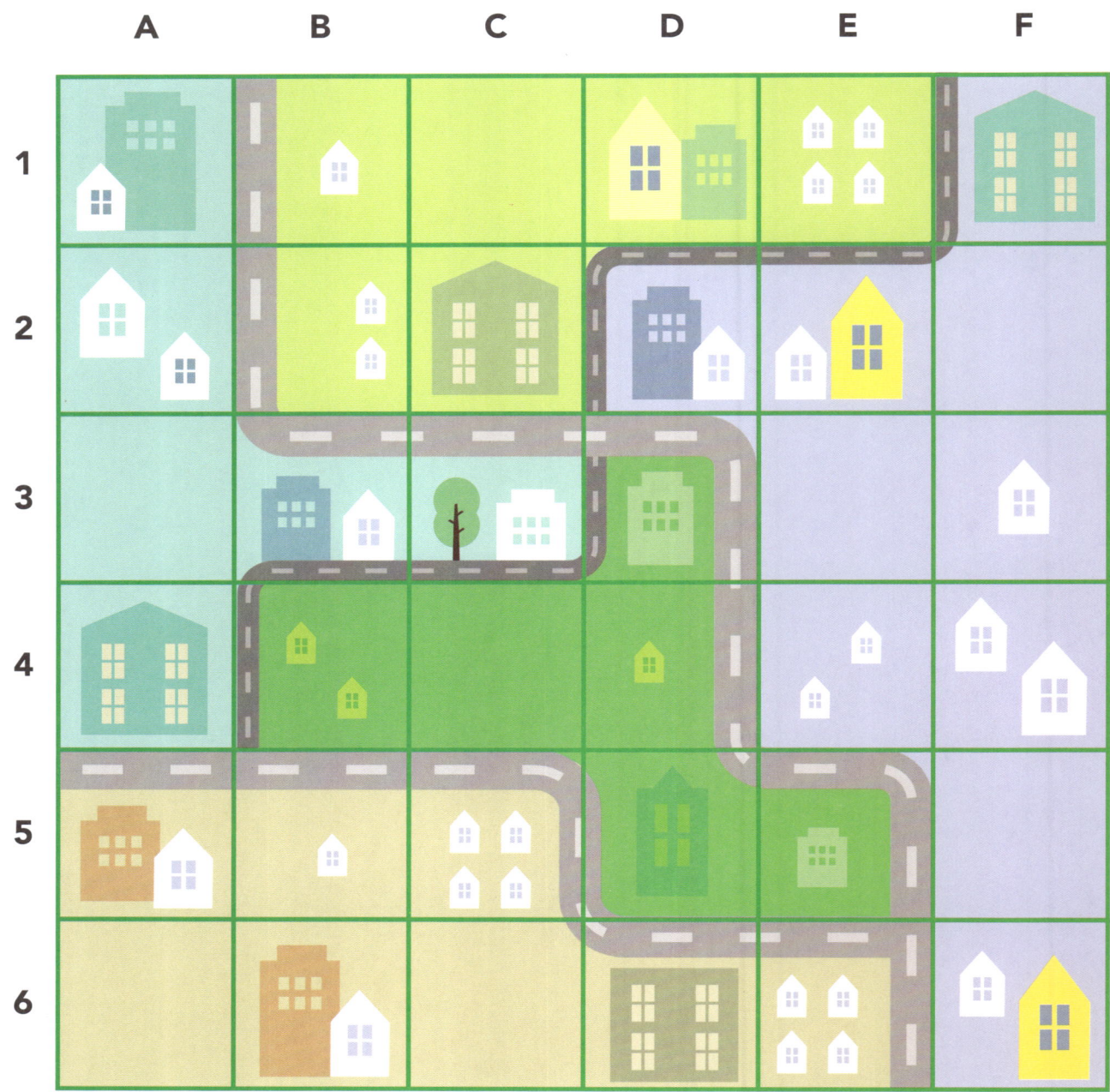

COMPLETE THE RESIDENTIAL DISTRICT WITH STICKERS, FOLLOWING THE COORDINATES.

A 6

LIBRARY

F 5

FIRE STATION

A 3

BUS STATION

C 6

CAFE

C 4

PARK

C 1

HOUSE

E 3

POLICE STATION

F 2

NEWSSTAND

The Suburban Area

THE AREA FURTHEST FROM THE CITY CENTER IS CALLED THE **SUBURBAN AREA**, AND IT IS DIVIDED INTO 3 DISTRICTS:

- **residential,** with houses, apartments, and sports centers.
- **commercial,** with parking lots, shopping malls, and warehouses.
- **industrial,** with factories, industries, and airports.

Connect each suburb to the correct definition.

COMMERCIAL DISTRICT

INDUSTRIAL DISTRICT

RESIDENTIAL DISTRICT

NOW DRAW A SUBURBAN AREA. USE THE STICKERS TO COMPLETE THE INDUSTRIAL, COMMERCIAL, AND RESIDENTIAL DISTRICTS IN THE BOXES BELOW.

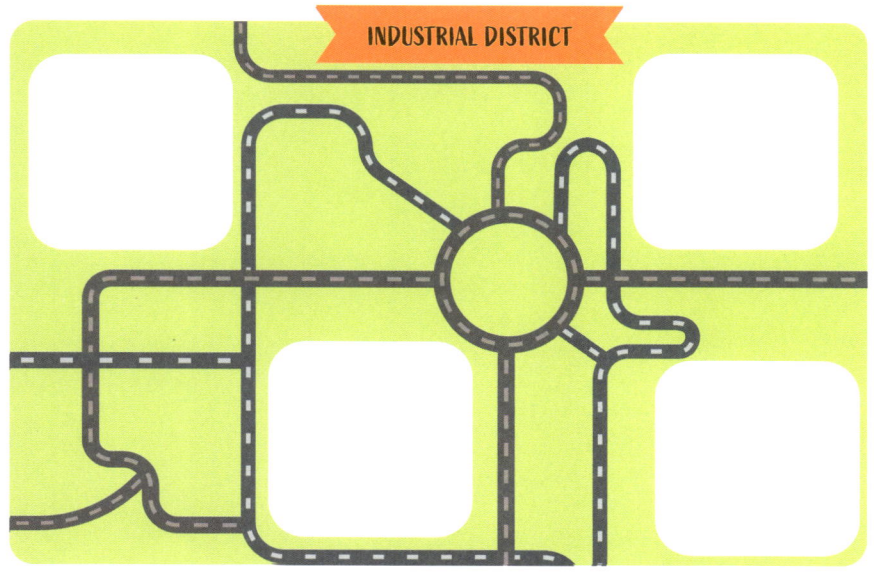

INDUSTRIAL DISTRICT

REMEMBER WHICH ELEMENTS CHARACTERIZE EACH DISTRICT!

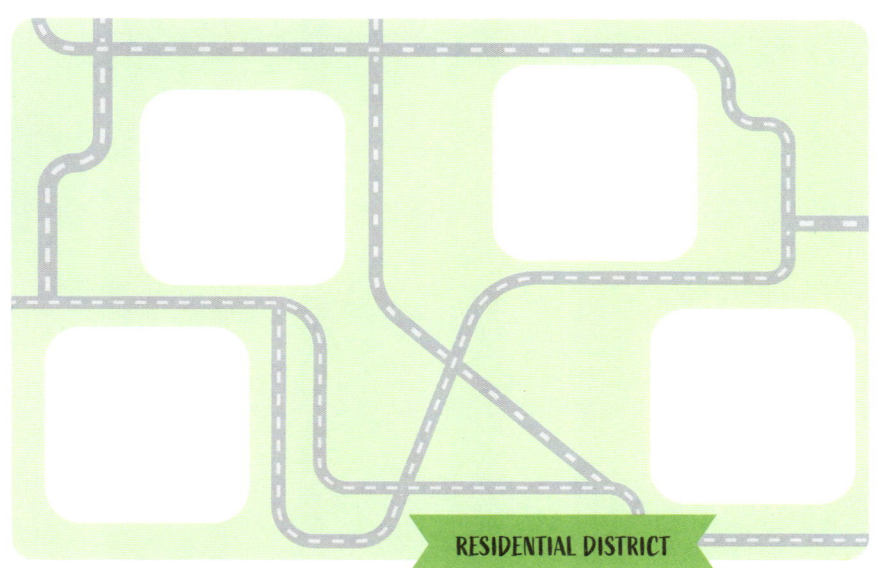

RESIDENTIAL DISTRICT

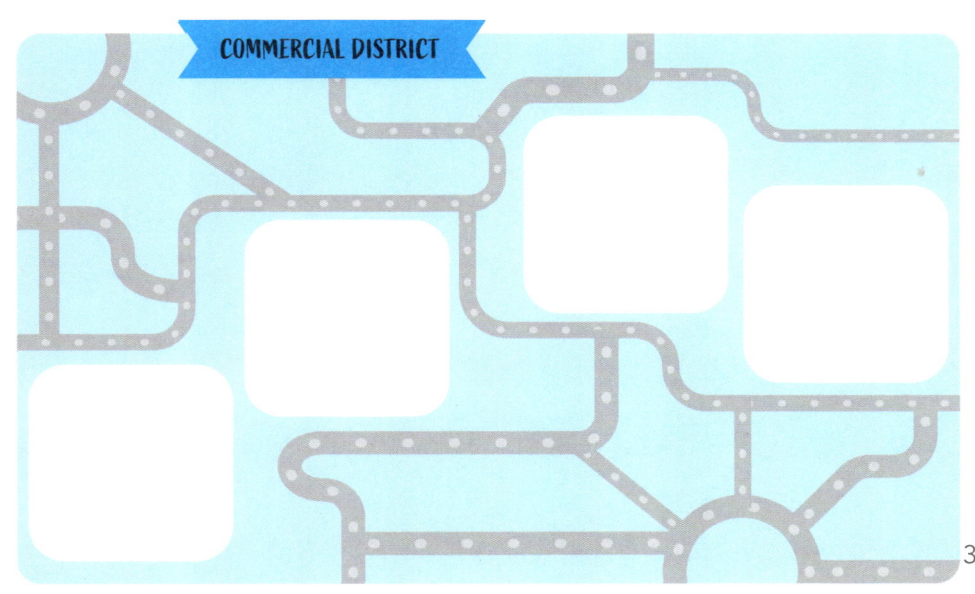

COMMERCIAL DISTRICT

Where Do You Live?

THERE ARE MANY TYPES OF PLACES WHERE YOU CAN LIVE.

Gea lives in an apartment, and Corby lives in a high-rise. Complete the various types of housing with stickers, then write their names in the correct place. Finally, circle the types of housing Tom, Gea, and Corby live in.

I LIVE IN A DETACHED HOUSE!

HUT   CAMPER   STILT HOUSE   CASTLE   TREEHOUSE   HIGH-RISE
APARTMENT   DETACHED HOUSE   CABIN

IGLOO

....

....

....

Homes for All Tastes

1. VIETNAM: Stilt houses stand above the water thanks to a wooden platform.

2. KENYA: The houses of the Masai are called **enkang** and are made of mud and dung.

3. GREENLAND: Houses are often on stilts to insulate them from the cold.

4. ITALY: In Alberobello there are **trulli**, which are conical-shaped houses made of stone.

5. NORTH AMERICA: A **tepee** was the typical Native American conical-shaped tent; it was made of animal skins, bark, or cloth.

6. MONGOLIA: A **yurt** is a portable home made with wood, sheepskins, blankets, and felt.

7. ARGENTINA: The traditional Argentine home is called a **casa chorizo** and has a rectangular plan; all the rooms are in a row.

8. JAPAN: Japanese **minkas** are wooden houses with rice paper doors.

9. DUBAI: Burj Khalifa is the tallest building in the world.

36

THERE HAVE BEEN SOME VERY SPECIAL HOMES IN THE WORLD. COME AND TAKE A LOOK AT SOME OF THEM WITH ME!

To find out where they are, put the stickers on the map following the numbers indicated in the key.

10. NETHERLANDS: Houseboats are only attached to land by a jetty.

11. PAPUA NEW GUINEA: Kombai people live in houses built in the treetops

12. MEXICO: a **Chukal Na** is the typical home of the Tzotzil people; it has a conical roof.

A DIY City

WOULD YOU LIKE TO HELP US BUILD A 3-DIMENSIONAL CITY?

YOU WILL NEED

- Cardboard boxes of various sizes
- Different colored tempera paints
- Markers
- Glue
- Masking tape

HOW TO MAKE THE CITY

1

The first thing we need to build is the city center and its buildings. Choose some different-sized boxes, then close them using glue and tape.

2

Paint them however you like, then decorate them with markers, adding windows, bricks, and writing. Next make the buildings in the residential district, such as homes, schools, a library, and a post office.

3

Finally, create the suburban area, using larger boxes that will become industries, hospitals, and shopping malls.

DON'T FORGET THAT THE OLDEST BUILDINGS AND MOST IMPORTANT MONUMENTS ARE FOUND IN THE CITY CENTER, SO DECORATE THE BOXES ACCORDINGLY!

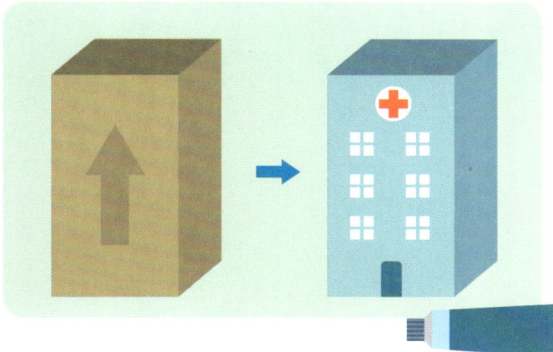

4

Now that you've made all the buildings, it's time to position them in a precise order: the city center buildings go in the center of our city; then place those of the residential district around them; finally, position those of the suburban area.

5

You've created a beautiful city! You can also add more details to make it even more realistic, such as parks, traffic lights and road signs, and vehicles.

THIS IS THE CITY THAT TOM, CORBY, AND I MADE.

Public or Private Transportation?

THERE ARE LOTS OF DIFFERENT MEANS OF TRANSPORTATION WE CAN USE TO GET AROUND THE CITY. SOME ARE PUBLIC, LIKE BUSES OR SUBWAYS, WHILE OTHERS ARE PRIVATE, LIKE MOTORCYCLES OR CARS.

Look at the pictures of the various means of transportation and circle the ones that are public.

I PREFER PUBLIC TRANSPORTATION: IT'S MORE SUSTAINABLE FOR THE ENVIRONMENT!

What Goes Where?

EACH MEANS OF TRANSPORTATION MUST USE ITS OWN ROUTE.

Connect the means of transportation to the correct lane.

BE CAREFUL NOT TO GET CONFUSED!

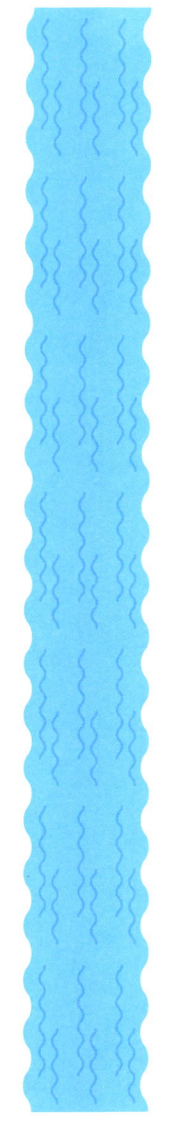

Find the Way

MANY CITIES HAVE A VERY LARGE SUBWAY SYSTEM.

Help Gea, Tom, and Corby find the fastest way to reach their destination by following the different colored lines. Will they have to change lines at a point of intersection?

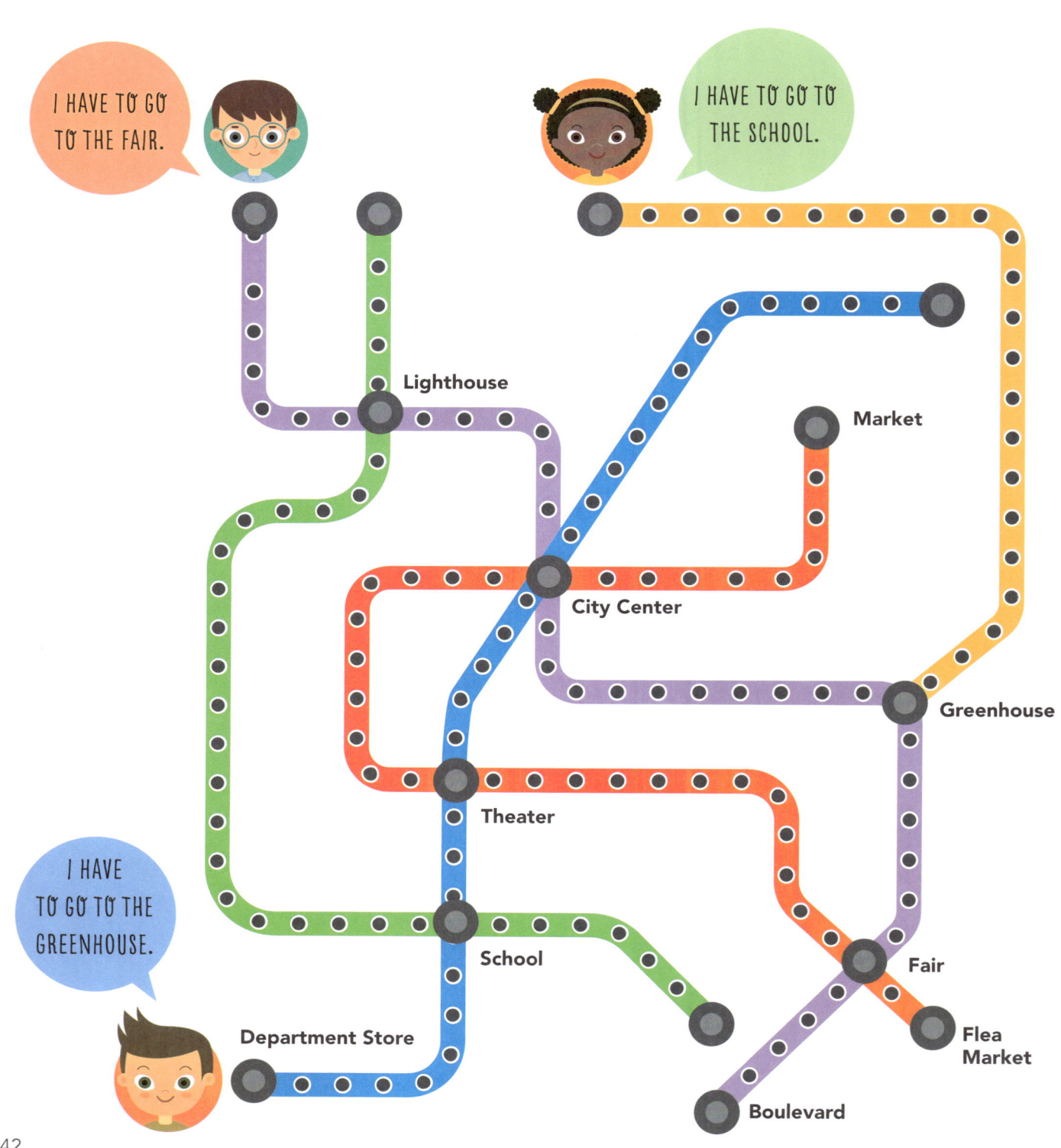

Signs and Signals

MEANS OF TRANSPORTATION FOLLOW ROAD SIGNS TO GET AROUND. DO YOU KNOW ANY?

There are three in each row, but only one is correct. Help me find the right ones!

WHICH SIGN MEANS STOP?

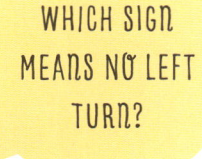

WHICH SIGN MEANS NO LEFT TURN?

WHICH TRAFFIC LIGHT MEANS YOU CAN GO?

Hidden Networks

IN ADDITION TO THE NETWORK OF ROADS AND COMMUNICATION ROUTES, THERE ARE ALSO UNDERGROUND NETWORKS THAT DISTRIBUTE WATER AND ELECTRICITY TO THE POPULATION.

Help the water droplet and the electricity get to the house through the two pipe mazes, avoiding the obstacles as you go.

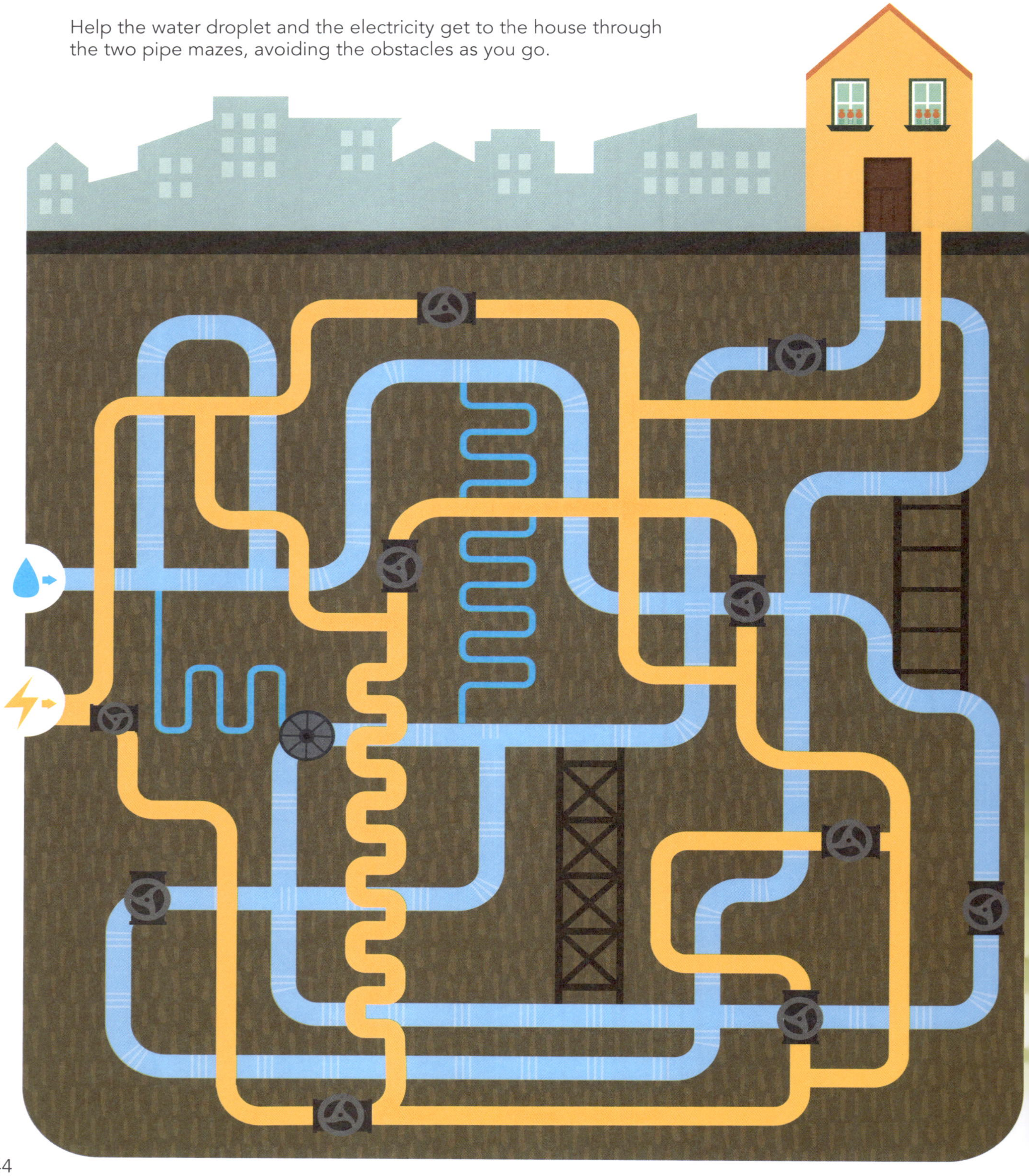

An Eye on Energy

WE USE ELECTRICITY FOR LOTS OF DEVICES WE USE EVERY DAY.

For example? Our computer, refrigerator, cell phone, microwave, television...

WHICH SWITCH TURNS THE LIGHT ON?

1 2 3 4 5

What a Racket!

CITIES ARE FULL OF SOUNDS...SOMETIMES VERY LOUD AND IRRITATING ONES!

More Sustainable Cities

WE SHOULD PAY MORE ATTENTION TO ENVIRONMENTAL ISSUES AND MAKE CITIES MORE SUSTAINABLE.

There are several ways to do this:

- making buildings that **consume less energy**
- using **renewable sources** such as **solar or photovoltaic panels**
- **recycling** waste
- avoiding **food waste**
- using **sustainable means of transportation** like **electric cars** and **buses**
- creating more **bike paths**
- reducing **water consumption**
- creating more **parks** and **gardens**

LET'S MAKE OUR CITY MORE SUSTAINABLE! TRANSFORM THE WRONG BEHAVIORS INTO CORRECT BEHAVIORS BY ATTACHING THE STICKERS, AS SHOWN IN THE EXAMPLE.

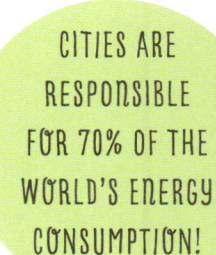

CITIES ARE RESPONSIBLE FOR 70% OF THE WORLD'S ENERGY CONSUMPTION!

WASTING WATER → WATER SAVING

TRAFFIC →

POLLUTING FACTORIES →

CITY WITHOUT GREEN AREAS →

WASTE →

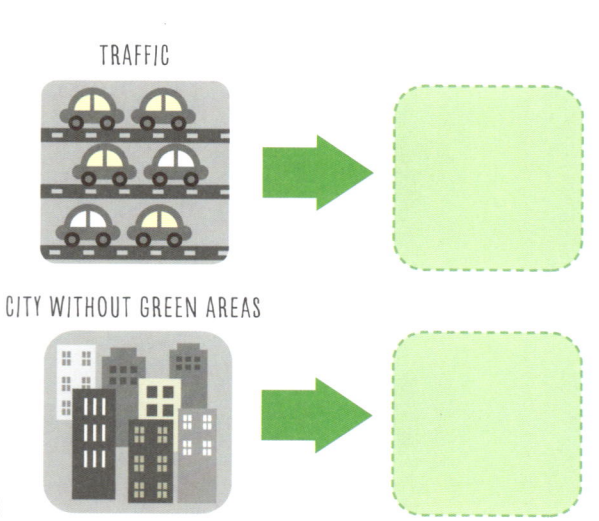
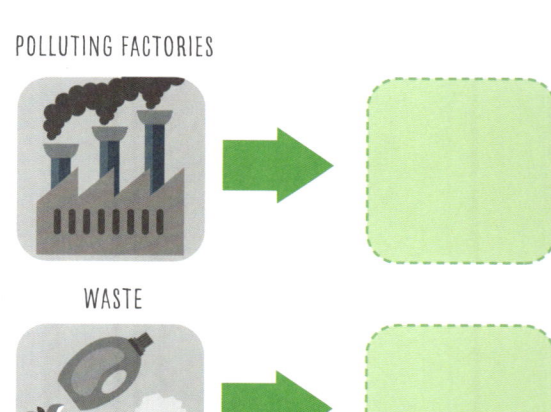

A Trip to the Future!

I LIKE THINKING ABOUT WHAT MY CITY WILL BE LIKE IN THE FUTURE.

How will we get around? Will there still be buses and trains? This is how I imagine it!

WHAT WILL HOUSES BE LIKE? WHAT ABOUT PARKS?

HOW DO YOU IMAGINE YOUR CITY IN THE FUTURE? DRAW IT BELOW.

The Urban Planner's Quiz

WE NOW KNOW LOADS OF THINGS ABOUT CITIES!
ANSWER THE QUESTIONS BELOW TO BECOME AN **APPRENTICE URBAN PLANNER.**

If you're not sure, use the book to help you!

1. Cities with more than 10,000 inhabitants are called **metropolises**. T F

2. **Demography** is the science that studies **populations** and how they change. T F

3. **Global cities** are cities that perform key functions for the global economy. T F

4. Cities in which the streets intersect at right angles are called **checked cities**. T F

5. A **suburban area** is the area of a city that's furthest from the city center. T F

6. **Sustainable cities** pay attention to reducing water consumption and food waste. T F

Check the answers at the back of the book.
If you've answered at least 3 correctly...
congratulations, you're now an apprentice urban planner!

color your ribbon!

color your ribbon!

If you got less than 3 right, try taking the quiz again!

Cities Memory Game

LET'S PLAY WITH CITIES IN THIS FUN MEMORY GAME!

Stick the stickers at the back of the book onto a piece of cardboard, then cut them out.
There are **48 tiles** and **24 pairs**.
Now you're ready to play with a friend!

Spread them out with the pictures facing down, then take turns turning over two tiles at a time. If a player finds two matching pictures, they keep the tiles and go again. If the tiles are different, they turn them back over and it's the other player's turn.
The game ends when there are no tiles left.
The winner is the person to have collected the most pairs!

Answers

PP. 6-7 SPOT THE DIFFERENCES

There are **14 differences**: wind turbine, dam, electricity pylons, dock, factory, cabins, playground, castle, hospital, train station and railroad tracks, museum, road, and barn.

PP. 8-9 RURAL OR URBAN?

P. 10 LET'S PUT EVERYTHING IN ORDER

P. 11 FIND THE NAME: MEGALOPOLIS

U	R	B	A	N	P	L	A	N	N	E	R	
M	E	T	R	O	P	O	L	I	S	●	●	
V	I	L	L	A	G	E	●	●	●	●	(M)	
(E)	I	N	H	A	B	I	T	E	D	●	●	
(G)	(A)	R	U	R	A	L	●	●	(L)	O	P	
●	C	O	U	N	T	R	Y	S	I	D	E	
B	U	I	L	D	I	N	G	S	●	●	●	
G	E	O	G	R	A	P	H	Y	●	●	(O)	
(L)	(I)	(S)	P	L	A	I	N	●	●	●	●	

P. 13 METROPOLITAN AREA

Which services are found only in the metropolis?
Airport, shopping mall, train station, theater.

P. 14 HOW MANY OF US ARE THERE?

1. The situation hasn't changed over time. — F
2. Today, the low-density area is smaller than it was in the past. — T
3. In the past, the high-density area was larger than it is today. — F
4. Today, the medium-density area is the same as it was in the past. — F
5. The low-density area was larger in antiquity. — T

P. 15 A MATTER OF LINES

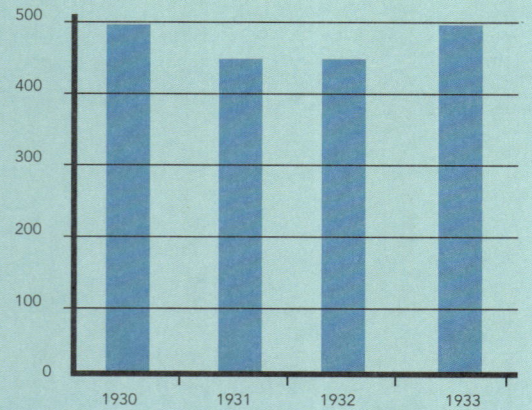

P. 16 A MATTER OF NUMBERS

400 INHABITANTS
Fari
Nima
Ulpe

6,500 INHABITANTS
Buka
Kandu

145,000 INHABITANTS
Turban
Mikkom
Gossy
Bandy

3,000,000 INHABITANTS
Dorty
Meddias
Megal

P. 17 IT'S NOT ALL ABOUT NUMBERS!
GLOBAL CITIES

PP. 18-19 CITIES OVER TIME

P. 20 THE FUNCTIONS OF A CITY

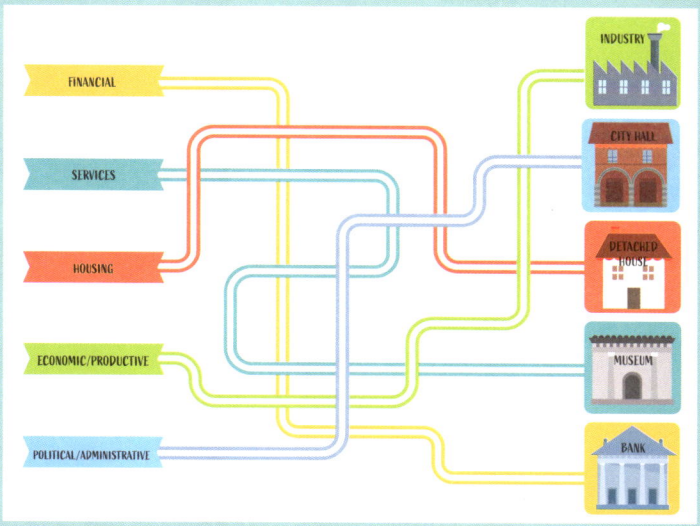

P. 21 PUBLIC OR PRIVATE?

PP. 22-23 WHERE AM I GOING?

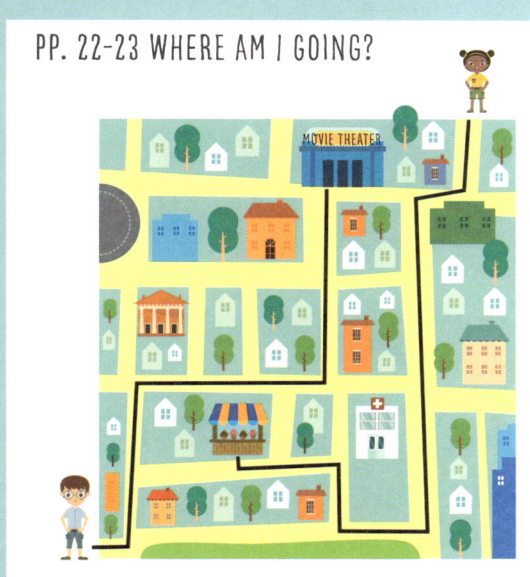

PP. 24-25 THE CITY TETRIS

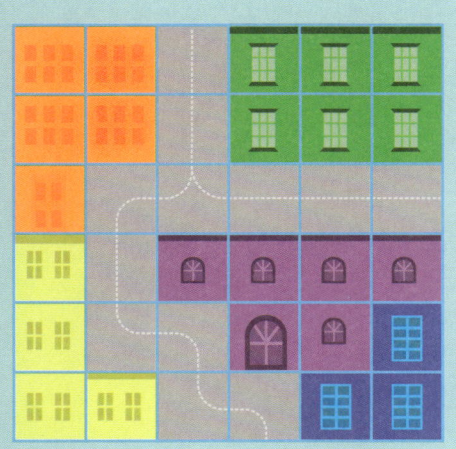

P. 26 DIFFERENT PATTERNS

P. 27 THE CITY CENTER

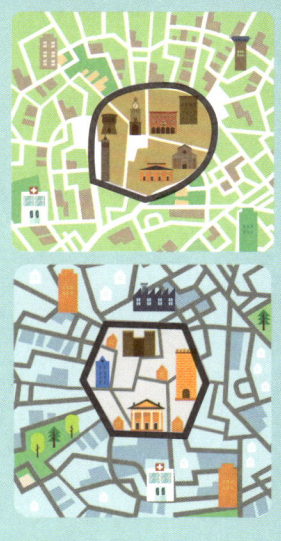

PP. 28-29 FAMOUS MONUMENTS

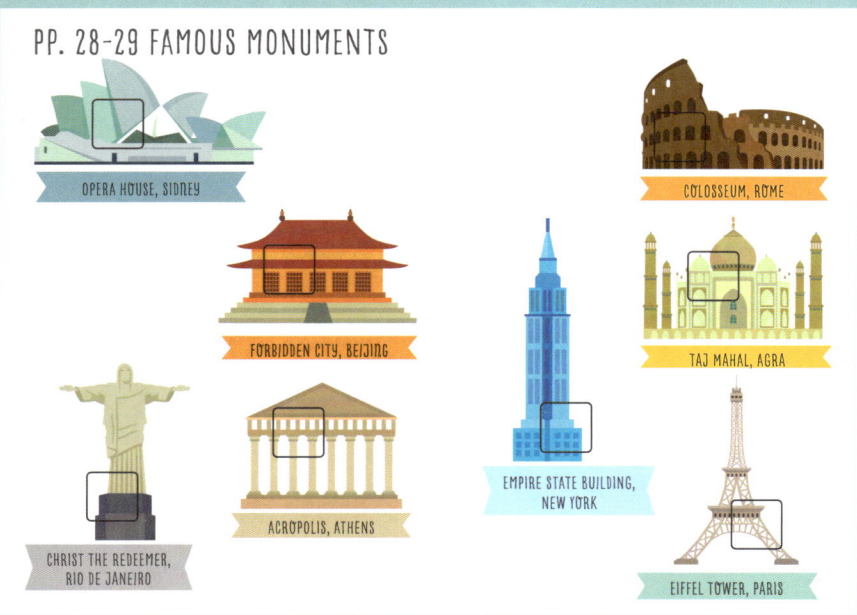

OPERA HOUSE, SIDNEY
COLOSSEUM, ROME
FORBIDDEN CITY, BEIJING
TAJ MAHAL, AGRA
CHRIST THE REDEEMER, RIO DE JANEIRO
ACROPOLIS, ATHENS
EMPIRE STATE BUILDING, NEW YORK
EIFFEL TOWER, PARIS

PP. 30-31 RESIDENTIAL DISTRICTS

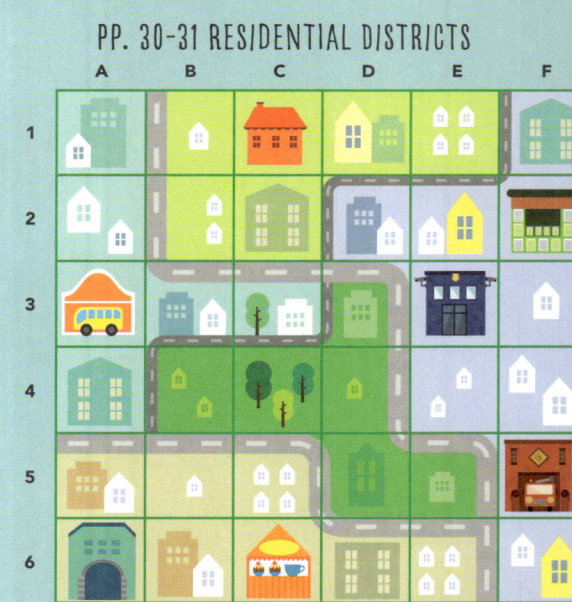

PP. 32-33 THE SUBURBAN AREA

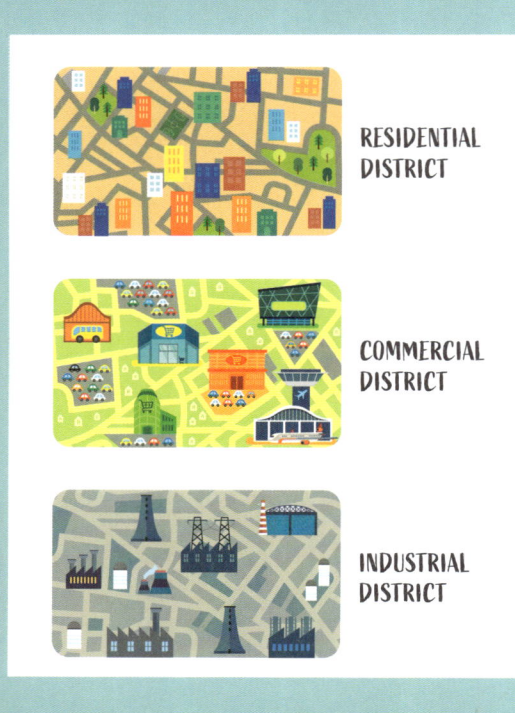

RESIDENTIAL DISTRICT
COMMERCIAL DISTRICT
INDUSTRIAL DISTRICT

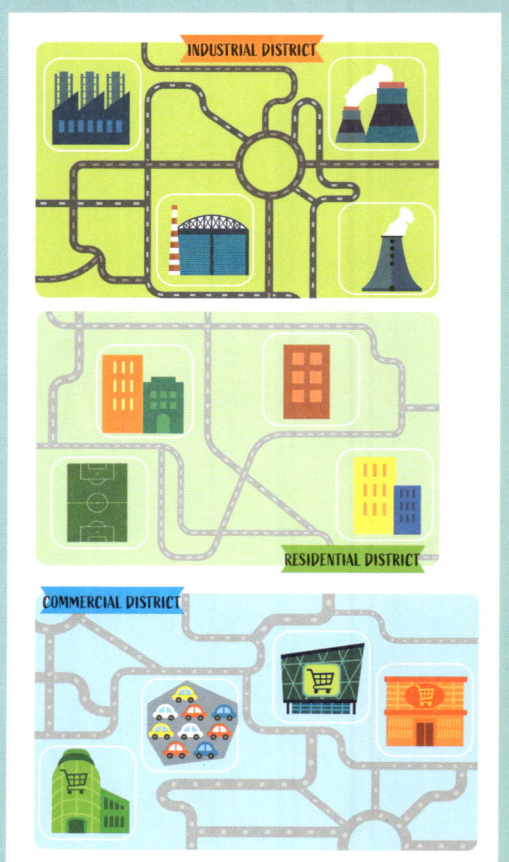

INDUSTRIAL DISTRICT
RESIDENTIAL DISTRICT
COMMERCIAL DISTRICT

PP. 34-35 WHERE DO YOU LIVE?

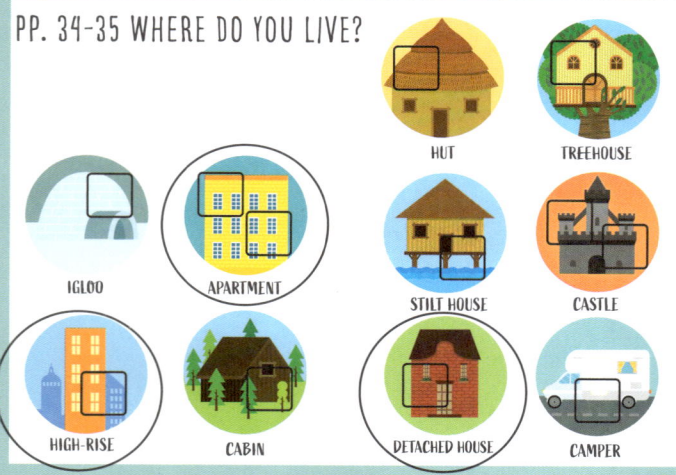

HUT
TREEHOUSE
IGLOO
APARTMENT
STILT HOUSE
CASTLE
HIGH-RISE
CABIN
DETACHED HOUSE
CAMPER

PP. 36-37 HOMES FOR ALL TASTES

P. 40 PUBLIC OR PRIVATE TRANSPORT?

P. 41 WHAT GOES WHERE?

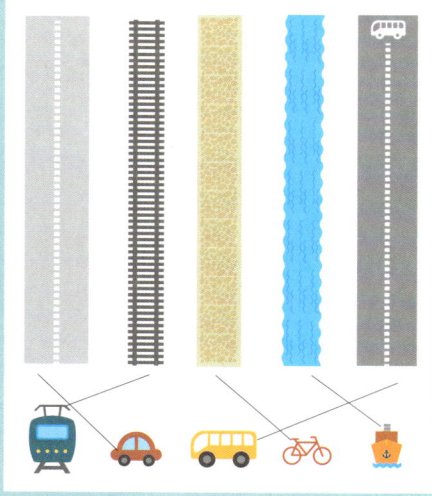

P. 42 FIND THE WAY

Gea takes the yellow line to the Greenhouse, then changes and takes the purple line to the City Center, then changes and takes the blue line to the **School**.

Tom takes the blue line to the City Center, then changes and takes the purple line to the **Greenhouse**.

Corby takes the purple line, which goes directly to the **Fair**.

P. 43 SIGNS AND SIGNALS

P. 44 HIDDEN NETWORKS

P. 45 AN EYE ON ENERGY

PP. 46-47 WHAT A RACKET!

P. 48 MORE SUSTAINABLE CITIES

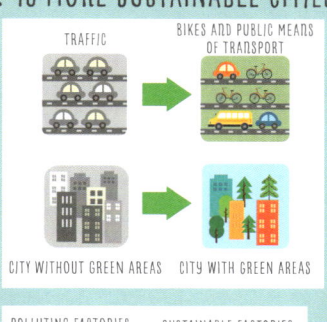

P. 50 THE URBAN PLANNER'S QUIZ

1. Cities with more than 10,000 inhabitants are called **metropolises**. F
2. **Demography** is the science that studies populations and how they change. T
3. **Global cities** are cities that perform key functions for the global economy. T
4. Cities in which the streets intersect at right angles are called **checked cities**. F
5. A **suburb** is the area of a city that's furthest from the city center. T
6. **Sustainable** cities pay attention to reducing water consumption and food waste. T

Paola Misesti

Paola was born in Como, Italy, in 1970, and has been living in Zurich, Switzerland, with her family since 2011. She is an educator who teaches Italian to foreign students, and she has also written and cowritten educational creativity and design books. She has been training educators, teachers, and parents for many years and does workshops and educational projects in kindergartens and elementary schools. For the past 10 years, she has been sharing her experiences and materials online, on her website, homemademamma.com.

Agnese Baruzzi

Agnese has a degree in graphic design from ISIA (Institute of Higher Education in the Artistic Industries) in Urbino, Italy. Since 2001, she has been working as an illustrator and author. She has created numerous children's books both in Italy and abroad. She holds workshops for children and adults, collaborating with schools and libraries. Over the past few years, she has illustrated many books for White Star Kids.

White Star Kids™ is a trademark of White Star s.r.l.

© 2023 White Star s.r.l.
Piazzale Luigi Cadorna, 6
20123 Milan, Italy
www.whitestar.it

Translation: TperTradurre S.r.l., Rome
Editing: Michele Suchomel-Casey

All rights reserved. No part of this publication may be reproduced, stored or transmitted in any form or by any means without written permission from the publisher.

First printing, September 2023

ISBN 978-88-544-2026-7
1 2 3 4 5 6   27 26 25 24 23

Printed and manufactured in China
by Allied Fortune Times Limited
(AF printing), Beijing, China

PP. 8-9 RURAL OR URBAN?

   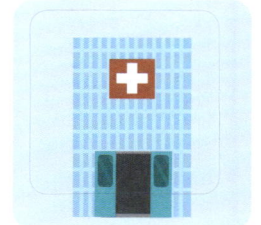

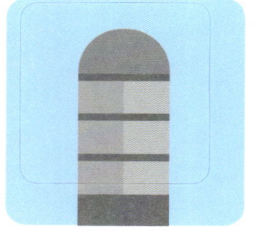   

P. 10 LET'S PUT EVERYTHING IN ORDER

P. 13 METROPOLITAN AREA

PP. 18-19 CITIES OVER TIME

 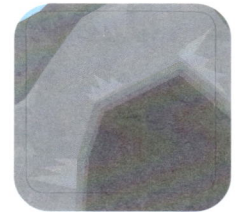  

P. 20 THE FUNCTIONS OF A CITY

P. 21 PUBLIC OR PRIVATE?

P. 21 PUBLIC OR PRIVATE?

  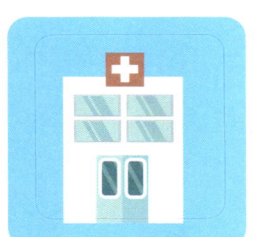 

PP. 24-25 CITY TETRIS

pp. 24-25 CITY TETRIS

p. 26 DIFFERENT PATTERNS

pp. 28-29 FAMOUS MONUMENTS

p. 30 RESIDENTIAL DISTRICTS

PP. 32-33 THE SUBURBAN AREA

   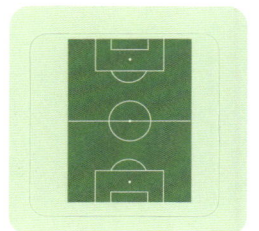

PP. 34-35 WHERE DO YOU LIVE?

PP. 36-37 HOMES FOR ALL TASTES

PP. 46-47 WHAT A RACKET

P. 48 SUSTAINABLE CITIES

P. 51 CITIES MEMORY GAME

  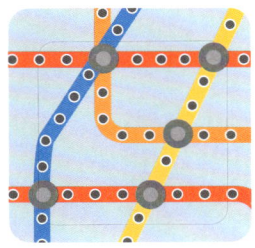 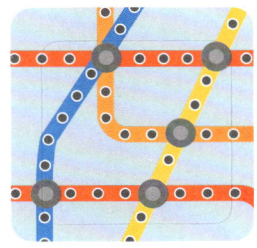

P. 51 CITIES MEMORY GAME

  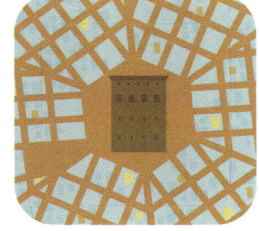 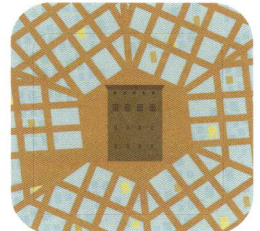